Korean Americans

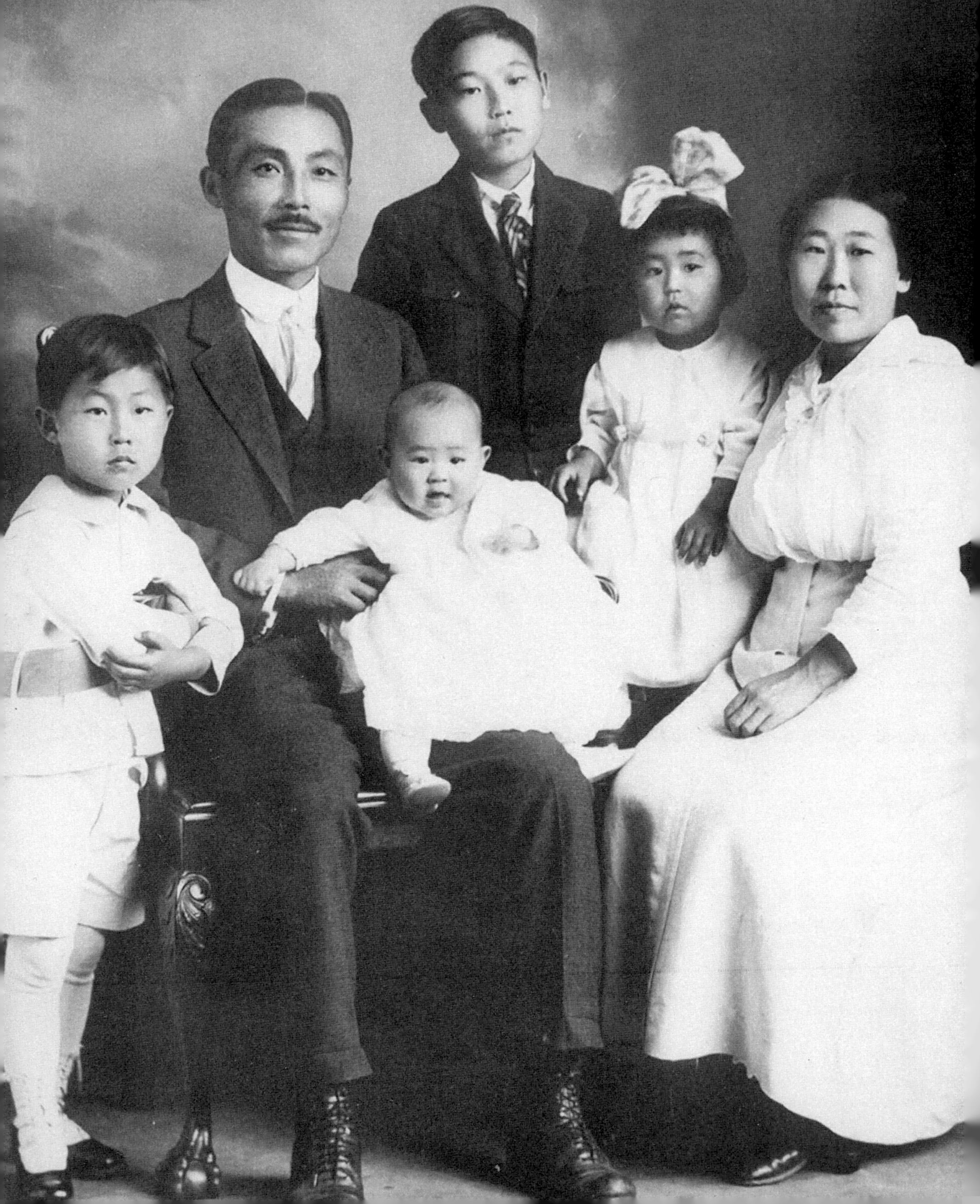

SPIRIT
of America®

Korean AMERICANS

By Cynthia Klingel

Content Adviser: Dr. Wayne Patterson,
Department of History, St. Norbert College

The Child's World®
Chanhassen, Minnesota

7

Korean AMERICANS

Published in the United States of America by The Child's World®
PO Box 326 • Chanhassen, MN 55317-0326 • 800-599-READ • www.childsworld.com

Acknowledgments
The Child's World®: Mary Berendes, Publishing Director

For Editorial Directions, Inc.: E. Russell Primm, Editorial Director; Sarah E. De Capua and Pam Rosenberg, Line Editors; Elizabeth K. Martin, Assistant Editor; Olivia Nellums, Editorial Assistant; Susan Hindman, Copy Editor; Joanne Mattern, Proofreader; Matthew Messbarger, Ann Grau Duvall, and Deborah Grahame, Fact Checkers; Tim Griffin/IndexServ, Indexer; Cian Loughlin O'Day, Photo Researcher; Linda S. Koutris, Photo Selector

Photos
Cover/frontispiece: Korean American Heritage

Cover photographs ©: Michael Newman/PhotoEdit

Interior photographs ©: Bettmann/Corbis: 9, 17, 26-top, 27; Ciniglio Lorenzo/Corbis Sygma: 26-bottom; Corbis: 11 (Lee Snider), 18 (Michael Kevin Daly), 21 (Rick Gomez), 22 (Jose Luis Pelaez, Inc.), 23 (Robert Landau), 24 (Christopher Felver); EMI Classics and Jazz, North America: 25; Getty Images/Tim Boyle: 28; Korean American Heritage: 7, 8, 12, 13, 14, 15, 16, 19.

Library of Congress Cataloging-in-Publication Data
Klingel, Cynthia Fitterer.
  Korean Americans / by Cynthia A. Klingel.
    p. cm. — (Spirit of America)
Includes index.
Contents: Leaving Korea—Life in America—Three Korean Americans today—Korean impact on American life.
  ISBN 1-59296-016-2 (Library Bound : alk. paper)
  1. Korean Americans—Juvenile literature. [1. Korean Americans.]
  I. Title. II. Series: Spirit of America (Child's World (Firm)
  E184.K6K55 2003
  973'.04957—dc21
                                    2003004292

12   17   22

Contents

Leaving Korea

THE PEOPLE OF AMERICA CAN TRACE THEIR **heritage** to countries all over the world. Immigrants—people who come from other countries—have been coming to America for hundreds of years. Immigrants from Korea began arriving in America in the 1800s.

Korea is a mountainous **peninsula** that sticks out of the continent of Asia. It borders on the northeastern part of China. It is about 600 miles (965 kilometers) long and only 125 to 160 miles (201 to 257 km) wide. Throughout Korea's history, other countries have fought for control over it. By the early 1900s, **natural disasters** and government corruption made life difficult for the Korean people. Most were poor, and there were few jobs. Looking for a better life, many Koreans began to leave their homeland.

In 1885, a small group of Korean men tried to take over the Korean government. They failed and fled to the United States for protection. These men became the first known Korean immigrants to the United States. In 1902, the Korean emperor Kojong gave his approval for ordinary Koreans to leave the country.

When Koreans began leaving their country, many believed they would return. Some thought they could go to America, make their fortunes, and then go back to Korea. So they went to work on Hawaiian sugar **plantations** where they were promised $15 every month, free housing, health care, and English lessons. American sugar planters wanted to hire them because they thought Koreans would be good workers and would accept very little in pay.

Between 1903 and 1905, there were 7,843 Koreans settled in America, mostly in Hawaii. Only 677 women and 465 children were part of this first wave of immigrants. They were

In 1902, Korean emperor Kojong gave his permission for ordinary Koreans to leave their country.

▶ As a peninsula, Korea was physically isolated from other countries, so it was known as the hermit kingdom.

The Koreans were badly mistreated when the Japanese took over Korea.

often treated badly in their new country. Over the next several years, fewer Koreans came. Japan took control of Korea during this time. The Japanese were cruel to the Korean people. Koreans were forced to speak Japanese, to work in factories, and to change their Korean last names to Japanese ones. They were also forced to cut their hair, which was a symbol of their religious beliefs. Japanese control angered Koreans. Many decided to leave.

This brought on the second wave of Korean immigration, which lasted from 1910 to 1924. More than 1,000 Koreans came to the United States. Most of them were women. The Korean men who had come to America earlier wanted to marry only Korean women. But there were few Korean women in the United States. The men began sending their pictures to friends and relatives in Korea. Their friends and relatives would show the pictures to Korean women and arrange marriages. The marriages would be approved, and the Korean brides would leave home and join their new husbands in America. These women were known as picture brides.

The American government passed the Immigration Act of 1924. This act was also known as the Exclusion Act. It made it nearly impossible for people from Korea and other Asian countries to come to America to live.

South Korean women and children greeting U.S. soldiers during the Korean War

It wasn't until the Korean War (1950–1953) that the next wave of Korean immigration began. Some of those allowed in were children whose parents were killed in the war. Others were Korean women who had married American soldiers stationed in Korea during the war. Often, these Korean women brought along relatives to live with them in the United States. But the Exclusion Act still kept most Koreans from entering America.

In 1965, the U.S. government passed the Immigration Act, making it easier for Koreans to come to the United States. By then, Korea was split into two countries, North Korea and

Interesting Fact

▶ Before 1900, only about 50 Korean immigrants had settled in the United States.

9

South Korea. Although the war had ended, the political and economic situation in South Korea was difficult. The United States and Korea created new agreements about how people could move to and from their countries. These changing factors encouraged Koreans to move to the United States. The result was a huge wave of Korean immigration.

From 1976 to 1990, between 30,000 and 36,000 Korean immigrants arrived each year. But these immigrants had different reasons for moving to America than those who came before them. They wanted a better life and better education for their children. Many of these immigrants were from upper-class Korean families. They were skilled workers with education and experience in science and technology.

Korean immigration was highest in 1987; since then, it has declined. In 1992, there were riots in Los Angeles. Many Korean businesses were destroyed. In 1994, only 10,799 Koreans entered the United States. That number has continued to decline, mostly because living conditions in South Korea have improved.

KOREA WAS DIVIDED IN 1945 AT THE END OF WORLD WAR II. MILITARY forces from the Soviet Union controlled the North, and American military forces controlled the South. Different governments were established in 1948. They couldn't agree on terms for bringing the country back together.

North Koreans were joined by Chinese soldiers and South Koreans were joined by American soldiers in a war for control that lasted from 1950 to 1953. Neither side could claim victory, and a peace agreement was signed in 1953.

North Korea is slightly smaller than the state of Mississippi. The capital of North Korea is P'yongyang. More than 22 million people live in North

Korea. Korean (left) is the official language, and the government is communist. Unlike South Koreans, residents of North Korea have only limited travel privileges within the country and are not allowed to travel to other countries.

South Korea is slightly larger than the state of Indiana. Its population is more than 48 million.

Korean is the official language, and the government is a republic. The capital of South Korea is Seoul. In June 2000, an important meeting took place between the leaders of North and South Korea. They signed a declaration to work toward improving relations between the two countries. Kim Dae-Jung, president of South Korea, won the Nobel Peace Prize in December 2000 for his commitment to democracy and human rights.

Chapter TWO

Life in America

AMERICA'S FIRST KOREAN IMMIGRANTS ARRIVED to work on the sugar plantations of Hawaii. They worked in the hot sun six days a week for 10 hours each day. They had few breaks. Often they were too tired to attend their English lessons when they weren't working.

The Korean workers developed their own leadership and set their own rules. This kind of self-government was called dong-hoe. Dong-hoe leaders from different plantations came together and formed the United Korean Society. The

A group of Korean farm workers in Sacramento, California, in 1913

society had branches all over Hawaii. In 1907, the society began publishing a newspaper called *The United Korean.*

Some Korean immigrants in the early 1900s did not settle in Hawaii but went to the United States **mainland** to work on railroads or grow rice and vegetables. Over time, more Korean societies, or organizations, were formed to offer support to other immigrants. The Korean Women's Association was formed in San Francisco in 1908. The Korean National Association was started one year later. It joined the United Korean Society in Hawaii with Korean organizations in California. Originally, it helped defend two Korean immigrants accused of assassinating an American who worked for the government of Japan, which controlled Korea at that time. They convinced the U.S. government to deal with the KNA instead of with the Japanese government on issues involving Korean Americans.

When the picture brides arrived, life for Korean immigrants changed. Families were

The United Korean *newspaper, published for Koreans in America*

13

Churches, such as this Korean Methodist Church in Oakland, California, were used by Korean immigrants for worship and as community centers.

established. They began having children. Many of the brides convinced their husbands to leave farming and move to cities where they would earn more money and where their children could go to school. In the cities, women took low-paying jobs in clothing factories that had poor working conditions and long hours.

About one-third of the Korean immigrants were Christian. They founded churches that became community centers where they could mingle with each other. These were also the places where immigrants could escape **discrimination.**

White Americans did not see Korean immigrants as being different from Chinese or Japanese Americans. They were all discriminated against as one large group.

In 1906, a San Francisco judge ruled that children from these three immigrant groups could not attend schools with white children. In 1913, California lawmakers passed the Webb Heney Land Law. This law said that Asian Americans could not own land. Discrimination was especially bad in San Francisco. White Americans there were afraid they would lose their jobs to Korean, Japanese, and Chinese Americans, who were willing to work for lower wages.

Immigrants also faced huge differences between their **culture** and American culture. Not only was the language different, but beliefs and values were different. This was hard for the immigrants to accept. The Korean organizations played an important role in helping them adjust to their new lives.

A group of Korean-American children in Riverside, California

15

Koreans were not allowed to immigrate to the United States between 1924 and the Korean War. However, the Korean American community continued to grow as the first immigrants started families. Their children began to adapt to American culture. Unlike other ethnic groups, such as Chinese and Japanese immigrants, Korean immigrants did not usually return to their home country. This is because Japan was still in control of Korea. Many Korean Americans worked for Korean independence from Japan.

Most of the first Korean immigrants came from cities. When they moved to America, they worked hard to move to American cities.

Korean-Americans often started their own businesses because discrimination made it difficult to find jobs.

16

White Americans often did not want to give them jobs in these cities. So many Korean Americans started their own small businesses, such as grocery stores. When World War II (1939–1945) began, industries in Hawaii and on the West Coast of the

A lot of the Koreans who immigrated to the United States during and after the Korean War were women who had married American soldiers.

United States needed workers. Many Korean Americans found jobs in these industries. They were thrilled when Korea was liberated from Japanese rule at the end of the war.

Many of the Koreans who were allowed to immigrate to America during and after the Korean War were women who had married American soldiers. They often confronted prejudice when they arrived in the United States. Often they found life on military bases very lonely. Some Americans adopted Korean children whose parents had died during the war. Some Korean children were abandoned

After 1965, many Koreans
came to the United States
to get a college education.

Interesting Fact

▶ The Korean War was
one of the most violent
in history. More than
560,000 international
and South Korean troops,
as well as 1.6 million
communist troops,
were killed, wounded,
or reported missing.
Approximately one
million South Korean
civilians were killed and
several million lost
their homes.

in the difficult time following the war. Many
of them were also adopted by American
soldiers or civilians and were allowed into the
United States.

Life for Korean immigrants who arrived
after 1965 was different from life for the earlier
Korean immigrants. The later immigrants were
better educated. They came from middle-class
and upper-class Korean families. Many of
them were in the United States to attend
college and to get good jobs. Some already had
advanced skills in science and technology.
Many were doctors and nurses hired by **inner
city** hospitals. These immigrants settled in the
suburbs rather than in the country or in
Korean neighborhoods in the cities.

18

AFTER JAPAN TOOK CONTROL OF KOREA IN 1910, many Korean Americans believed that Korea should fight for independence. They organized efforts in the United States to prepare Koreans for war with Japan. Groups were formed that raised money and provided skills, knowledge, and political support to the people of Korea.

Some Korean Americans started a School of Aviation where they trained other immigrants to be fighter pilots. They had fund-raising campaigns sponsored by organizations such as the Korean National Association. Park Yong-man (left) led the Korean Youth Corps, a voluntary military training school in Hastings, Nebraska. Its goal was to train immigrants to assist in gaining Korea's independence.

Even when Korea gained its independence from Japan after World War II, these groups continued to send money, food, clothing, and other aid to the people of Korea.

Chapter THREE

Korean Americans Today

Interesting Fact

▸ Between 1970 and 1980, 600 Korean "green groceries" opened in New York City.

KOREAN AMERICANS HAVE MADE AN IMPACT on the United States. In several cities, Korean businessmen turned old, boarded-up buildings into clean, attractive businesses. In New York City, Korean "green grocers" selling fresh flowers, fruits, and vegetables have become popular and can be found in almost every neighborhood.

In fact, Korean Americans have become very successful in business. In Chicago, most of the dry cleaning stores are owned by Korean Americans. In New York, Los Angeles, and El Paso, Texas, Korean Americans run successful **import** and **export** businesses.

Korean-American children often do well in school and have excelled in national science scholarship competitions. Their

Korean-American "green grocers" sell flowers, fruits, and vegetables in New York City.

parents have high expectations for them.

One difference between the Korean and American cultures is the role of women. In the Korean culture, women are not expected to work outside the home. However, Korean-American women have needed to work to help support their families. Today, these women are becoming **activists** who help other Korean-American women deal with the problems of working outside the home.

Most Korean Americans today are Christian. Christian missionaries in Korea

▶ Korean immigrants
entered the United States
in such great numbers
after 1965 that it was
difficult to track them.
In 1980, it was esti-
mated that there were
three times more Korean
Americans than the
Census Bureau had
on record.

often introduced the American culture to Koreans and helped them immigrate. Churches are still important places that provide opportunities for them to find support with language, culture, jobs, and housing.

Korean-American life is not always happy. Korean Americans have had to confront racism. The divorce rate for Korean Americans has been higher than in Korea. Korean-American women are most likely to be divorced. Many of these women were married to American soldiers. Korean Americans, like other Americans, have had to deal with all kinds of practical problems. However, the Korean people are survivors. They know how to change and endure. They find support through strong churches and community organizations. They are hard workers who are committed to success in the United States.

A Korean-American mother showing a family photograph to her sons

In 1990, Korean Americans in New York City started the Center for Korean American Culture. The purpose of the center is to provide a place for young Korean Americans to share their experiences and struggles with one another, as well as share their culture with others in the United States.

The center offers programs that build pride among Korean Americans in

their heritage. It also helps them develop skills to be successful. The center supports many arts activities including songs, dances, festivals, films, and crafts. It also organizes workshops about Korean culture.

One way the Korean culture is shared is through a performing group called Shinmyung Pae. Experts from Korea taught this group how to perform Poongmul, the traditional music and dance of Korea. Poongmul is performed sitting and standing. Instruments accompany the dancelike movements. The group performs to educate others and to celebrate Korean holidays.

23

Korean Impact on American Life

Nam June Paik is a famous Korean-American artist.

KOREAN AMERICANS HAVE FOUND SUCCESS IN American arts, government, sports, and entertainment. One of the first Korean artists in the United States was Whanki Kim, who lived in New York City from 1963 until his death in 1970. Kim was known for the bright colors he used. The bright reds and greens came from traditional colors that were used to paint Korean temples. His work was described as being Asian in style with a mysterious quality. Another famous Korean-American artist is Nam June Paik. He settled in New York

Sarah Chang is a world-famous violinist who began playing violin as a young child.

and was known for using televisions in his art.

Sarah Chang, the daughter of Korean immigrants, began performing violin when she was five years old. At age six, she began taking lessons at the famous Juilliard School of Music. She played as a guest violinist with the New York Philharmonic Orchestra by age eight. Since then, she has played with other famous orchestras throughout the world.

Younghill Kang was a writer and professor at New York University. He wrote of his

Korean-American author Younghill Kang was also a professor at New York University.

experiences as a child living in Korea during Japanese control. His first novel was *The Grass Roof,* published in 1931. Americans read this and learned what it was like to live in Korea and to suffer under the Japanese.

Herbert Choy, a Korean American, became the first Asian American to be named to a federal court. President Richard Nixon appointed him to the U.S. Court of Appeals in 1971. In 1992, California

Margaret Cho is a popular comedian who has performed on television and in movies.

Sammy Lee is a Korean-American diver who won two Olympic gold medals.

businessman Jay Kim became the first Korean-American member of Congress.

Many Americans watched Korean-American comedian Margaret Cho in the 1994 television show *All American Girl.* Cho continues to perform stand-up comedy.

In sports, Korean American Sammy Lee won a gold medal in diving in both the 1948 and 1952 Summer Olympic Games. In 1992, Eugene Chung joined the New

England Patriots football team. Byung-Hyun Kim is a pitcher for the Arizona Diamond-backs, a major league baseball team. Kim pitched in the 2001 World Series.

For more than 100 years, Korean Americans have worked hard to be recognized as an ethnic group that is separate from other Asian groups. Individually, they have shown determination, patience, and commitment to becoming successful members of American life.

Members of the Korean-American Association of Chicago participating in a Memorial Day parade in that city

28

1903–1905   Over 7,000 Koreans settle in America, most in Hawaii.

1906   A San Francisco judge rules that Korean, Chinese, and Japanese children cannot attend school with white children.

1908   The Korean Women's Association is founded in San Francisco, California.

1909   The Korean National Association is formed.

1910   Japan takes control of Korea, setting off a wave of Korean immigration to the United States that lasts until 1924.

1913   The Webb Heney Land Law is passed in California, making it illegal for Asian Americans to own land.

1924   The Immigration Act of 1924, also known as the Exclusion Act, makes it nearly impossible for Koreans and people from other Asian countries to come to the United States.

1945   Korea is divided into North Korea and South Korea at the end of World War II.

1950   The Korean War begins.

1953   The Korean War ends and the country remains divided.

1965   The Immigration Act is passed, making it easier for Koreans and other Asians to immigrate to the United States.

1971   Herbert Choy, a Korean American, becomes the first Asian American appointed as a federal court judge.

1987   More Koreans come to the United States than in any other year.

1992   Jay Kim becomes the first Korean-American member of the U.S. Congress.

activists (AK-teh-vests)
An activist is someone who takes direct, enthusiastic action in support of or in opposition to an issue. Today, some women are becoming activists who help other Korean-American women deal with the problems of working outside the home.

culture (KUL-chur)
Culture is the ideas, skills, arts, tools, and way of life of a certain people at a certain time. Immigrants faced huge differences between their culture and American culture.

discrimination (dis-KRIM-in-a-shun)
Discrimination is the practice of treating certain groups of people unfairly or unequally because of an unreasonable dislike or distrust of them. Churches and community centers were places where immigrants would not face discrimination.

export (EX-port)
To export is to send goods from one country to another for sale. In New York, Los Angeles, and El Paso, Texas, Korean Americans run successful import and export businesses.

heritage (HAIR-ih-tij)
Heritage is something that is handed down from one's ancestors or from the past, such as skills or traditions or a way of life. The people of America can trace their heritage to countries all over the world.

import (IM-port)
To import is to bring goods into one country from another for sale. In New York, Los Angeles, and El Paso, Texas, Korean Americans run successful import and export businesses.

inner city (IN-er SIH-tee)
The sections of a large city in or near its center that are usually older, poorer, crowded and in bad condition. Many Korean doctors and nurses were hired to work at inner city hospitals.

mainland (MAIN-land)
The mainland is the main part of a country or continent, separate from its nearby islands. Some Korean immigrants went to the United States mainland to work on railroads or grow rice and vegetables.

natural disasters (NAH-chur-al dih-SAS-terz)
Natural disasters are something in nature that causes much damage or suffering, such as a flood or earthquake. In the early 1900s, natural disasters made life difficult for the Korean people.

peninsula (peh-NIN-su-la)
A peninsula is a piece of land that sticks out from a larger piece of land and is almost completely surrounded by water. Korea is a mountainous peninsula.

plantations (plan-TA-shunz)
Plantations are large farms, usually in a warm climate, on which crops are grown by workers who live there. America's first Korean immigrants lived on the sugar plantations of Hawaii.

suburbs (SUH-burbs)
A suburb is a smaller community on the outskirts of a city but far from its center, with mostly homes and little or no industry. Korean immigrants settled in the suburbs rather than in the country or in the Korean neighborhoods in the cities.

For Further INFORMATION

Web Sites

Visit our homepage for lots of links about Korean Americans:
http://www.childsworld.com/links.html

Note to Parents, Teachers, and Librarians:
We routinely verify our Web links to make sure they're safe,
active sites—so encourage your readers to check them out!

Books

Orr, Tamra. *The Korean Americans.* Philadelphia: Mason Crest Publishers, 2003.

Park, Frances, Ginger Park, and Yangsook Choi (illustrator). *Good-Bye, 382 Shin Dang Dong.* Washington, D.C.: National Geographic Society, 2002.

Peterson, Tiffany. *Korean Americans.* Chicago: Heinemann Library, 2003.

Places to Visit or Contact

Korean American Museum (KAM)
P.O. Box 741879
Los Angeles, CA 90004
213/388-4229

Korean Cultural Center
5505 Wilshire Boulevard
Los Angeles, CA 90036
323/936-7141

Index

About the Author

CYNTHIA KLINGEL HAS WORKED AS A HIGH SCHOOL English teacher and an elementary school teacher. She is currently the curriculum director for a Minnesota school district. Cynthia Klingel lives with her family in Mankato, Minnesota.